WISCONSIN

A PICTURE MEMORY

Text
Bill Harris

Captions
Fleur Robertson

Design
Teddy Hartshorn

Photography
Richard Hamilton Smith
Colour Library Books Ltd
FPG

Picture Editor
Annette Lerner

Commissioning Editor
Andrew Preston

Editorial
Gill Waugh
David Gibbon
Pauline Graham

Production
Ruth Arthur
Sally Connolly
David Proffit
Andrew Whitelaw

Director of Production
Gerald Hughes

CLB 2677
© 1991 Colour Library Books Ltd., Godalming, Surrey, England.
All rights reserved.
This 1996 edition is published by Crescent Books,
a division of Random House Value Publishing, Inc.,
40 Engelhard Avenue, Avenel, New Jersey 07001.

Crescent Books and colophon are trademarks of Random House
Value Publishing, Inc.

Random House
New York • Toronto • London • Sydney • Auckland
http : / /www. randomhouse.com/

Printed in Hong Kong
ISBN 0-517-06026-4
12 11 10 9 8 7 6

WISCONSIN
A PICTURE MEMORY

CRESCENT BOOKS
NEW YORK / AVENEL, NEW JERSEY

Whenever the roll of the states is called, Wisconsin is always second from last, but there is never any question about its right to be on the list. It has been there since 1848 and getting there wasn't easy. For a while it looked as though the Badger State might be compromised out of existence by neighbors chipping away at its boundaries before it had a chance to be born.

When it was established as a Territory in 1836, Wisconsin included all of Iowa and Minnesota, as well as a chunk of the Dakotas, along with its present territory. But in an earlier incarnation it had also included a stretch of the lower shore of Lake Michigan that included the trading post known as Chicago. When Illinois became the twenty-first state, Wisconsin had no status in Washington and no way to protest the politician's call for a port on the Great Lakes. Thirty years later, when Michigan applied for statehood, the Wisconsin Territory did have representation in the national government, but it wasn't powerful enough to fight off a compromise that gave the Wolverine State the top of the peninsula that looks even to the most casual map reader as though it ought to be part of Wisconsin. The giveaway was granted because Michigan claimed it had been cheated out of territory when Ohio became a state nearly forty years earlier. It wasn't as though the Territorial Legislature at Madison didn't protest, or that it didn't offer compromises, but all the pleading fell on deaf ears. It did, on the other hand, give them a platform for a call to statehood. The people weren't convinced it was such a terrific idea, and it took two tries to come up with a constitution they could agree on. But they finally did accept the proposition of becoming one of the United States, probably in the nick of time. When talk of statehood reached the St. Croix Valley, the people there said they wanted no part of it and fought hard to push the Wisconsin line further east. They lost in the end when the St. Croix River became the new state's northwestern boundary. But Wisconsin lost, too. The original plan had been to push the line west to follow the Mississippi River right from its source.

If all that weren't enough, when the American government established itself on the banks of the Potomac River, there were more people living in the tiny District of Columbia than there were whites in all of Wisconsin, even within its old boundaries. And those who were there, largely in the Green Bay area, thought of themselves as French. The Americans had taken control of the area under the terms of the treaty that ended the Revolutionary War, but the British didn't bother to leave for another dozen years, and even then it was only a formality. To all intents and purposes the English went right on running things for yet another two decades, even though the American army was garrisoned there. And all the while, the people who lived between the British trading posts and the American forts went right on speaking French.

It would probably be a mistake to assume that they all got along happily even though there is no evidence of open hostility. The English have never hidden their feelings about the French, and in those post-Revolutionary years there were few Anglophiles among the Americans. But the people most affected by the conflict were the Indians, and some of them also found themselves caught up in the middle of the machinations of the Spanish.

In most parts of America misunderstandings between whites and Indians were usually the result of Europeans taking over traditional hunting grounds, but in Wisconsin the problem was quite different. At least it was in the beginning.

The first humans to leave their mark on the area arrived about fifteen thousand years ago, even before the great glacier that shaped the land had completely melted. They were followed by cultures known as mound-builders, who left behind earthworks that still dot the Wisconsin landscape in greater numbers than in any other part of North America. The Indians we traditionally regard as the original Americans arrived about a thousand years after the mound-builders, and slowly the two groups became almost interchangeable. By the time the French trappers arrived in the mid-seventeenth century, there was virtually no difference between the descendants of the mound-builders and Algonquins who had migrated into their midst from the north and east.

But there was another culture there, too. The Winnebago, who were relatives of the Sioux. Tribes from the south and west routinely attacked their villages and in time, thanks to wars and epidemics, the forests of Wisconsin had virtually no Indian population at all. But it was only a temporary situation. The Iroquois tribes east of the Great Lakes had been armed by Dutch and English trappers, and they used their guns to terrorize the Chippewa, Hurons and other Algonquin nations living in the Hudson Valley and deep into Canada. In about 1654, the Algonquin refugees began arriving in Wisconsin in numbers large enough to intimidate the remaining Winnebago into letting them stay.

The old wars with the Iroquois flared up again thirty years later. The Algonquin had been gathering furs for the French, the Iroquois preferred selling theirs to the English, and the competition provided all the reason any of them needed to go on the warpath. The Fox and several other Algonquin tribes used the war as an excuse to revolt against their French customers in favor of dealing with the English, who paid better prices. But the French were too powerful, and in the end they not only defeated them but dictated where they and all the other tribes in the area might live.

All of the tribes of both nations had fought for the French against the British at one time or another, but when the English finally took control, none of them seemed to have any problem serving their new masters. But when the American Revolution broke out some of them joined the rebels, even though the war itself was far off to the east and most Indians had strong personal reasons for not liking Americans in general. Still others offered their services to the Spanish, who were also at war with England, and who at the time controlled the territory to the west and south of Wisconsin. When the war was over and the Americans claimed the territory, one of their first affronts to the local population was to move four tribes intact from New York to Wisconsin.

The immigrants were encouraged to become joint owners of the land with the local Menominee, the oldest established Algonquin tribe in the area, and though the newcomers were their distant cousins, they were less than pleased by the arrangement. The situation simmered for a decade and then the Americans added insult to injury.

In 1830, a band of Sauk led by Chief Black Sparrow Hawk went home to their village after the winter hunt and found that it had become a white settlement while they were gone. Not only were their homes taken, but the graves of their ancestors, sacred to all Indian tribes, had been plowed under. Black Hawk held his peace and moved on to Canada to get the advice of the English about what he should do next. Naturally, they told him to go back and fight. When his men appeared on the horizon, the squatters called out the militia and Black Hawk and his people were driven across the Mississippi,

where the chief decided to resort to negotiation. But the Sioux who lived west of the river told him that they'd join his fight, and he led his people eastward again. The sight of five hundred Sauk warriors crossing the river terrified the white settlers and the militia was mobilized once again. Midway through their first encounter, Black Hawk organized a truce party which was massacred before the peace pipes could be produced. It served to enrage Black Hawk, who counterattacked and won the battle. That encouraged other raids and, as the casualties multiplied, the whites' defending army grew into the thousands and Black Hawk and his people were forced to retreat into Wisconsin. Two major battles were fought there as the Sauk tried to escape across the Mississippi, where their brothers still hadn't kept their promise to help. Black Hawk himself was captured, and his defeat sent a message to the other tribes that there was no hope of trying to stop the tide of white settlement. Nearly all of them left the territory.

The end of the Black Hawk War, which had been thoroughly covered in the eastern newspapers, served as a signal that Wisconsin was open for settlement. Within two years the land rush was on. It had been anticipated more than fifty years earlier, when the Continental Congress persuaded the old colonies to relinquish their claims to all the territory due west of their original land grants. The agreement, called the Northwest Ordinance, provided that lands north of the Ohio River would be carved into three to five new states as soon as the population had grown large enough. It was the reason why some of the other would-be states were able to dictate Wisconsin's borders. They had resolved their Indian problems sooner and had grown faster.

The earliest Wisconsin settlers were transplanted from the eastern states, mostly New York, and from Canada. But once statehood became a reality and railroads began opening the interior, immigrants from Germany and Scandinavia arrived and started cultivating wheat, which was the mainstay of the Wisconsin economy for more than thirty years. As the country moved westward many of the wheat farmers moved with it, but they were replaced by lumbermen and by farmers more interested in raising livestock than grain.

But there were better ways to make money in Wisconsin's early days. When the Territorial Government was established, the land itself was the future state's most important asset and far and away the best way to turn a profit. When all of it belonged to the Indians, the beneficent Americans agreed to pay them for it. The price was low, of course, but many an Indian brave gave up hunting and trapping when he discovered he could turn land into Yankee dollars. Whites got in on the action, too, and when the Territory was declared safe for civilization, a land boom resulted in some uncivil wheeling and dealing. Men with investments of a few hundred dollars saw the value escalate into the thousands almost overnight. And even those with no land to sell and no money to buy any found a way to turn a profit.

Land speculation was a national passion in the 1830s and many of its sharpest practitioners never bothered to leave their offices in New York or Philadelphia. They hired agents to do their buying for them, and the folks who actually owned the land colluded with them to unload parcels that were either too far from water to support settlement or so deep under water that nothing could ever be built there. But it still wasn't a game everyone could play. Most of the land in Wisconsin still belonged to the Federal Government, and it wasn't until a few years after granting territorial status that it decided to sell it at auction to the highest bidders.

During the months before the auction, would-be property owners in future towns and cities picked the lot of their dreams, and then signaled their intention to own it by building a shack and clearing away some of the trees. Theoretically, other bidders would respect their wishes and they could set their own price when the government auctioneer arrived. The theory was sound as long as neighbors respected each other's rights, which they almost always did. But outsiders presented a problem. They would arrive in a town on the morning stage dressed in their city finery and, after ceremoniously lighting a tasty cigar, they'd make the rounds, appraising the staked-out building lots. As soon as they were sure all the locals had noticed their presence, they'd approach one of the squatters and, after lavishly praising the shack, they would let it be known that it was exactly what they were looking for. They were so obviously well-heeled that the poor settler saw his dream about to be dashed with the knowledge that he could never compete with such resources at auction time. But before a tear could be shed, the stranger would offer to put aside his own dream for a small donation in the neighborhood of a hundred dollars. It was a lot of money, but it was obvious that the man could drive up the cost of the land well beyond that, and the settler usually scraped the bribe together. Sometimes the stranger was kind enough to loan it to him at a nice rate of interest. It was a nice racket. But like most rackets it had a fatal flaw: greed. Very few of the players were content with one or two extortions per town and usually put the arm on every squatter in a neighborhood. Worse, it was such an easy way to make money that many settlers were often approached by two or three such speculators, all with their hands out. Eventually the settlers rebelled and then they banded together. They refused to make any payments to anybody but the government agents, and backed up their resolve by showing up at the auctions in the company of their brawny neighbors. If any outsider bid against one of them, he was usually nowhere to be found when the auctioneer tried to pick him out of the crowd. As a result, very few parcels of land were sold for a penny more than the government's minimum asking price of $1.25 an acre. That's not to say it wasn't resold soon after for hundreds of dollars more. But the locals defended their sales by noting that there was no arm-twisting involved, and the buyers were usually city people anyway. Racketeering, then as now, was in the eye of the beholder.

Sometimes a little dishonesty made all the difference, in fact. In the 1860s a man drifted into Sparta, bought some land and buried drums of oil under it. At the turn of a spigot, he could cause just enough oil to flow to bamboozle prospective buyers. Before the hoax was uncovered, he drifted on with some $50,000 in his pocket. But when the buyers poked around for more oil, they discovered mineral springs instead and the town became a thriving health resort.

Even the Indians had favored the protected plain at the edge the Mississippi that the French trappers called *Prairie La Crosse*, and when immigrants began arriving from New York in the 1840s they agreed wholeheartedly that it was a perfect spot to start building a future city. It was well on its way by 1851, when it was made the county seat, with its own sawmill, a gristmill and even a weekly newspaper, not to mention three churches. In the years that followed it became a favorite destination for refugees from revolutions in Germany and Norway, and by mid-decade, with a population of more than 3,000, it dropped the word "Prairie" from its name and declared itself a city. Central to its plan for the future was the idea that a railroad was going to be built between La Crosse and Milwaukee, and most of the settlers and nearby farmers eagerly invested their savings in the scheme. They lost their money when the railroad company went bankrupt during the panic of 1857, but they didn't lose faith in La Crosse. The local businessmen began wearing their Sunday best every day of the week and went out to meet every arriving steamboat. They may have been down at the heels and with holes in their pockets, but they did such a fine job of making their city look prosperous that in a few years it actually was. The railroad was eventually built, and when the Civil War cut off traffic on the Mississippi it became the center of east-west traffic as well as a key manufacturing center. There were enough thirsty working men in La Crosse by the '80s that its four breweries were turning out more beer than any city in Wisconsin. Yes, more even than Milwaukee. But Milwaukee was catching up. The difference was that the beer barons on the lake were shipping about half their production to other states and, in the process, beer was making Milwaukee famous.

But Wisconsin has given America much more than a taste for beer. On the other side of the coin, it has more cows and produces more milk than any other state, not to mention more maple sugar than Vermont, good to know if you like sugar cookies with your milk. Wisconsin has given us John Dillinger the bank robber and John Muir the naturalist. It produced architect Frank Lloyd Wright and statesman Carl Schurz. It was the birthplace of the Ringling Brothers Circus and Harry Houdini, as well as Spencer Tracy, Alfred Lunt and Orson Welles. A Wisconsinite invented the safety razor, but probably the most unkind cut of all came from the state legislature that in 1911 gave Wisconsin the first state income tax in the nation. But the Wisconsin state government led by Robert LaFollette set a higher standard for other states to follow, and his ideas are still at work, not only in the Badger State but in most of the others as well.

The state motto is a simple one: "Forward." It's the only direction Wisconsin has known since its neighbors stopped chipping away at its borders a century and a half ago. All is forgiven now. After all, who could blame those other states from wanting to be part of Wisconsin?

Facing page: Port Wing on Lake Superior in the grip of winter.

These pages: farmland in rural southern Wisconsin, the state's most populous region, where the summer crops of hay, corn and oats go to feed the state's vast numbers of dairy cows. Wisconsin is the foremost producer of milk and cheese in the country; there are more cattle than people in the state. Overleaf: a spic and span farm near Monroe in the extreme south of Wisconsin. This part of the state has the best soils and the longest growing season – about six months. During the nineteenth century, after lumbermen had cleared the region's extensive forests, farmers moved in to settle and plant wheat, which, for most of the century, was Wisconsin's major crop. This gave way to dairy farming after cinch bugs damaged the wheat crop several years running and the need for agricultural diversification became clear.

Below: pleasure craft tucked up for the night on Geneva Lake (facing page top), southwest of Milwaukee in the south of the state. Facing page bottom: negotiating the hazards on the golf course of a major recreation area in Lake Geneva, a resort on Geneva Lake. Golf is only one of the sports available here – riding, hiking and cycling are among the others.

Wingspread (these pages), built in 1939 for the H. F. Johnson family in Racine, is the last and largest of Frank Lloyd Wright's "Prairie Houses." The living areas of the house stand above a raised basement of "Cherokee Red" brick (below); the cantilevered north wing is the only second level. The chimney in the eight-sided living room (remaining pictures) is set with a fireplace on each of its four sides. "We called the house 'Wingspread,'" wrote the architect, "because spread its wings it did."

Above: the Performing Arts Center in Milwaukee, the second largest city in the state, which boasts a variety of civic amenities, including Milwaukee County Stadium (facing page top), Mitchell Park Horticultural Conservatory (below and facing page bottom) – known as "the Domes" – and Milwaukee County Zoo (above left). The latter is one of the finest in the world, housing many animals which are endangered in the wild. Left: a through-the-hooves view of Milwaukee's Great Circus Parade and (below left) an outdoor event during Milwaukee's annual Summerfest, which takes place on the downtown lakefront during July and presents of a wide variety of musical performances.

18

19

The city of Milwaukee is dominated by the First Wisconsin Center tower (these pages and overleaf), home of the biggest bank in Wisconsin, from which it is possible to gain a superb view of Lake Michigan (facing page top) and the extremely flat land surrounding the city.

Below: the gleaming copper brew kettles of the Miller Brewing Company in the nation's beer capital, Milwaukee (left, below left and overleaf). More beer is produced here than anywhere else in the United States, but there is more to the city than brewing. The Performing Arts Center (above left and facing page top) and the Pabst Theater (above) serve the community with concerts and plays, while the Milwaukee Art Center and War Memorial has on permanent display one of the finest collections of European and American art in the country. For those more interested in energetic pursuits, the city's Convention Center is used for a wide variety of events, including the National Square Dancers' Convention (facing page bottom).

25

Old Wade House (these pages), in Greenbush, was built in 1851 as a stagecoach inn at the halfway point between Sheboygan and Fond du Lac once owned by Sylvanus Wade and his wife Betsy. The twenty-seven rooms of the interior, including each of the guest rooms (left), the parlor (below left) and dining room (bottom left), were restored in 1953 by the Koehler Foundation and the house dedicated as a state park.

The center of Madison (facing page and overleaf), the capital of Wisconsin, lies on an eight-block-wide isthmus between lakes Mendota and Monona in the south of the state. Below: the Beaux Arts style State Capitol, Madison, which was finished in 1917 after eleven years.

Below: Little Norway, a tourist attraction which comprises picturesque nineteenth-century homesteads full of Norwegian antiques near Mount Horge, south of Madison. Facing page: (top) a cheerful troll outside the Swedish store at Mount Horeb and (bottom) Old World Wisconsin.

These pages: the bizarre interiors of the House on the Rock complex near Dodgeville, one of Wisconsin's biggest tourist attractions. The complex is centered upon a stone mansion built by sculptor Alex Jordan on a chimney rock that towers 450 feet above the Wyoming Valley. The sculptor began his mammoth work in the 1940s, opening the house to the public in 1961. Within its rooms can be found such unexpected sights as trees growing though floors, waterfalls and pools, as well as a vast collection of musical instruments (bottom left) and a touch of New Orleans with a room decorated in the Vieux Carré style (below). In 1968 Jordan went on to build a Mill House to hold his vast collection of paperweights, dolls, armor and music boxes. Ultimately his vision included exhibits on circuses, Oriental arts, console theater organs and a giant carousel, as well as a recreation of a nineteenth-century street, the "Streets of Yesterday" (left). It takes a day to see all that is on show here – the product of one man's flair, determination and fascination with life.

37

Below: land flooded by the Wisconsin River near Boydtown, close to where the river meets the Mississippi in Wyalusing State Park (facing page bottom and overleaf) in the extreme southwest of the state. Facing page top: wooded hills and tranquil water near Lynxville, part of the Upper Mississippi River Wildlife and Fish Refuge on the Wisconsin border.

Below left: a farm near Galesville. Above left: fall colors reminiscent of a Vermont hillside in Devil's Lake State Park, which, like the Circus World Museum (left), a State Historical Site, lies near Baraboo in south Wisconsin. From 1884 until 1912, Baraboo was the winter quarters of the Ringling Bros. and Barnum and Bailey Circus – the five Ringling Brothers began their careers in the circus here. A few miles to the north of Baraboo lie the Wisconsin Dells (above, below and facing page) – fifteen miles of superb rock formations and one of the state's premier attractions. Overleaf: silver birch twigs and a solitary conifer highlight the colors of fall near Ontario, southeastern Wisconsin.

Facing page top: one of the many hundreds of lakes in Chequamegon National Forest, which contains trees that were once part of the famous Great North Woods. Above: an immaculate farm, and (above right) a family home in Lake Wissota State Park, both of which lie north of the city of Chippewa Falls on the Chippewa River (right). Below: a fisherman proudly holds up his catch at Old Chippewa City (below right). Facing page bottom: the Wisconsin winter holds farmland in its grip near Nelson, close to the Minnesota border in the east of the state, and (overleaf) mist rolling in across the autumn hills like the tide of some inland sea near the eastern town of Menomonie.

Facing page and below: peaceful woodland in Hartman Creek Recreation Area, which lies to the east of Waupaca in the center of the state. This recreation area boasts fourteen miles of hiking trails and a mile-long nature trail. Fishing is one of the most rewarding pastimes for visitors here: Wisconsin is thought to have over 10,000 lakes in all, and lakes and ponds are familiar sights along the highway. Above right: a roadside pond along Highway 51 at Whiting, south of Stevens Point, and (above) another south of Wisconsin Rapids. Right: the Grand Rapids of the Wisconsin River, looking as untamed as the day they were discovered. Below right: apple harvesters near Chippewa Falls.

Above left: safe harbor on Lake Michigan at Algoma, like Kewaunee (left), a town in Door County. Door County is a forty-two-mile-long peninsula on the east coast of the state renowned for its beauty; quaint coastal villages, such as Gills Rock (below left), have earned the county the nickname "Cape Cod of the Midwest," but sites such as unspoiled Kangaroo Lake (below) and a beach (facing page bottom) overlooking Death's Door on Lake Michigan give this part of Wisconsin a character all its own. Above: white-water rafting at Big Smokey Falls on the Wolf River in eastern Wisconsin and (facing page top) boating on Arrowhead Lake, near the town of Woodruff.

Below: a perfect winter's day heralds the start of the midwinter Ski Race in Hayward, a town in the northwest of the state which remains lively all year round. In July Hayward hosts the Lumberjack Days Festival and the Lumberjack World Championships (remaining pictures), when competitions in tree chopping, log rolling, tree climbing and sawing promote fierce rivalry between the top lumberjacks in the country. The event has been nationally televised in the past and attracts international contestants. The town continues the theme of wilderness taming in Historyland, a restored logging camp east of town that allows the visitor a glimpse of the life of the men who felled so much of the Great North Woods in the last century. It features a logging museum, an old railroad station, an original Haywood hotel and a cook's shanty where the visitor can eat his fill of lumberjack vittals. Overleaf: dramatically beautiful Big Manitou Falls, the state's largest waterfall, which forms the highlight of Pattison State Park in the extreme northwest of the state.

Facing page: (top) Brownstone Falls and (bottom) Cascade Falls empty into the Bad River Gorge in Copper Falls State Park, south of Ashland. The park is well supplied with trails to and footbridges across this spectacular gorge. Below: wild lupins bloom in profusion beside Highway 13 north of Washburn in Bayfield County, northern Wisconsin.

Above left: a glimpse of a sunset from one of Sand Island's caves. Sand Island is one of the Apostle Islands on Lake Superior, twenty-two of which lie within the Apostle Island National Lakeshore. The largest of the group is Madeline Island, formerly the site of one of the most important fur-trading posts in the North. Here lies Big Bay Island State Park (above and left) and Madeline Island Historical Museum (below and below left). Facing page bottom: the marina at La Pointe, Madeline Island, where passengers (overleaf) await the last ferry of the day to Bayfield (facing page top). Following page: a cheerfully painted barn north of Washburn in the north of the state.